T0157700

MOTHER
ARISE AND PRAY
Every Mother's Prayer Handbook

Mama

NEVER
STOP
Praying
FOR YOUR
Children

CHISA NOSAMIEFAN

WESTBOW
PRESS®
A DIVISION OF THOMAS NELSON
& ZONDERVAN

WestBow Press books may be ordered through booksellers or by contacting:

WestBow Press
A Division of Thomas Nelson & Zondervan
1663 Liberty Drive
Bloomington, IN 47403
www.westbowpress.com
1 (866) 928-1240

Because of the dynamic nature of the Internet, any web addresses or
links contained in this book may have changed since publication and
may no longer be valid. The views expressed in this work are solely those
of the author and do not necessarily reflect the views of the publisher,
and the publisher hereby disclaims any responsibility for them.

Any people depicted in stock imagery provided by Getty Images are
models, and such images are being used for illustrative purposes only.
Certain stock imagery © Getty Images.

ISBN: 978-1-5127-9827-2 (sc)
ISBN: 978-1-5127-9828-9 (hc)
ISBN: 978-1-5127-9826-5 (e)

Library of Congress Control Number: 2017912291

Print information available on the last page.

WestBow Press rev. date: 03/06/2020

ENDORSEMENTS

I first met Chisa Nosamiefan at a conference hosted by a dear, mutual friend in Philadelphia, Pennsylvania. I noticed two things about her instantly: her smile and her teenaged son who accompanied her. It was a women's conference and so I thought, "This kid must be so bored!" I mean, what kind of teenage boy wants to go to a Christian women's conference? But I soon realized he was a gem. He had driven her from Boston to Philadelphia so that she wouldn't have to drive alone. He was there simply to serve his mom. I then gave my testimony, about being single and celibate for over twenty years and it was her son who first approached me when I was done, telling me what an impact my story had on him! Not only didn't he mind being surrounded by (mostly) middle aged women, he actually listened and his heart was humble and soft enough to receive. I wanted Chisa's recipe! How could I raise my sons to be so respectful, so humble, so sensitive and, well, so *good*?

At last, Chisa shares this *recipe*. It is simply prayer: frequent, intentional passionate prayer, in a way that only a mother, or a grandmother can pray. Rather than worry, we moms can pray! And our fervent, effectual prayers will avail much (Jas 5:16). Younger moms, take note! Older moms, don't despair! God is able to do exceedingly abundantly beyond what we can ask or think, but it all starts in prayer (Eph 3:20). Thank you Chisa, for leading us.

Nicole Doyley
Author of *The Wait: Encouragement for Single Women*

The mother-child bond is incomparable to any other.

This is why when a mother prays for her child, she prays from a place of affinity and sympathy that makes her prayer effectual.

This book by Pastor Chisa Nosamiefan could not have come at a better time.

There is a spiritual battle raging for our children's lives and destinies. The devil is employing all kinds of means to derail our seed. And he is relentless!

Unfortunately many mothers are in a state of spiritual slumber (Mathew 13:25), which is why this book Mothers Arise And Pray is so timely. God does nothing except in response to prayer!

Pastor Chisa's passion for praying our children into their destinies is palpable in this book.

I wholeheartedly endorse and recommend this book to every mother who desires to position her children, through prayer in a place where they can fulfill God's plan for their lives.

Pastor (Mrs) Dele Bamgboye
Highflyers' Christian Centre
Port Harcourt, Nigeria.

Minister Chisa Nosamiefan is a committed, focused and experienced Christian woman, wife, mother and grandmother with deep concerns for children of all nations, regardless of race, creed, colour or ethnicity. I firmly believe that what she has to share in this prayer book is definitely needed in the Body of Christ and will also transform lives and be a blessing to many in nations throughout the world, all to the honour and glory of God.

I therefore, endorse her book, Mother Arise and Pray: A Mother's Pocket Prayer Guide and also highly recommend it to be a resource prayer book, especially for all intercessors.

Min. Hilda M. Douglas
Chairperson of Aglow International Caribbean Regional Committee and National Director, Northern Caribbean Area

My heartfelt honor to all mothers who labor to see their children reach their destiny in Christ.

O, my dear children! I feel as if I'm going through labor pains for you again, and they will continue until Christ is fully developed in your lives. (Galatians 4:19 ESV)

And to my amazing children Winchele, Dolo, and Y'osa, and my lovely grandchildren Chisa and Niger, who are my inspiration.

Children with good sense make their parents happy. (Proverbs 15:20a GNT)

Grandparents are proud of their grandchildren. (Proverbs 17:6a GNT)

CONTENTS

FOREWORD

It is no surprise to me that my friend and sister of nearly twenty years would finally put to print what God has birthed in her. I met her back in 1999 when she and her husband were serving as missionary pastors in Haiti, and she was the president of Haiti Aglow International. I have witnessed firsthand the powerful prayer ministry alive in Pastor Chisa. We have prayed together over these years for our own children and anyone else's children who have come into our awareness. As a mother of seven and grandmother of ten, I can emphatically state that this book is so timely as we consider the conditions we find in these last days. It not only charges the younger mother with young children or the more mature mother parenting teens but the seasoned mother with adult children as well. There is no exempt category here, and the book covers in-depth prayer topics, focus, remedies, and mainly scriptures to guarantee prayers are not being tossed out without purpose. I give praise to almighty

God for His continuous demonstration of love for us as He provides us a fresh perspective on waging war on behalf of our children through the lens of a seasoned prayer warrior, Pastor Chisa.

Minister Paulette Holloway, MSW, LICSW
All Nations Baptist Church Washington, DC
Author of *Tea With God: Everyday Encounters and Thieves Of Intimacy*

INTRODUCTION

The Lord began to prompt me to start a prayer meeting for mothers to pray for their offspring and this generation. I did not act on it right away; I procrastinated for many months till I had a vision on Mother's Day the following year.

I saw a long and wide highway with many children walking up and down and their mothers walking behind them. Suddenly, a dark cloud reached down and snatched a child. The mother screamed and chased after the cloud as it receded with the child in its grip. Within a split second, the child had disappeared, swallowed up in the cloud. The same thing repeated, child after child, till the mothers were left wailing and screaming in search of their children. It was horrifying. I was sobbing as this vision unfolded before my eyes. At that moment, I knew I must begin to assemble women to pray for their children, their grandchildren, and this generation. That was the birth of the Mother Arise and Pray movement.

Mother Arise and Pray is an intercessory prayer ministry mobilizing women to pray for their children and grandchildren via telephonic and online prayer meetings, prayer rallies in churches, women's ministry gatherings, in prisons, and in the wider community.

After two years of conducting daily prayer meetings, I was inspired to put together a collection of topical prayers that will help every mother pray effective scripture based prayers anytime they are burdened to pray.

Arise, cry out in the night, as the watches of the night begin; pour out your heart like water in the presence of the Lord. Lift up your hands to him for the lives of your children, who faint from hunger at every street corner. (Lamentations 2:19 NIV)

HOW TO USE THIS BOOK

Mother Arise And Pray: Every Mother's Prayer Handbook can be used individually or with a group of mothers. It could be used as a quick reference, a daily prayer guide, or a group prayer manual. It teaches how to pray by subject based on Bible verses.

STRUCTURE OF THE BOOK

There are twenty-one overarching prayer topics with a number of scriptures that address the particular subject and corresponding prayers. These prayers can be done as a twenty-one-day prayer initiative or as an in-depth group prayer program for twenty-one weeks.

The book begins with a guide to a mother's personal repentance before beginning to pray for her children. "*Repentance (metanoeo)* means to change one's mind for the better—to heartily amend with abhorrence of one's past wrongdoing." Thayer and Smith, "Greek Lexicon entry for Metanoeo" "The NAS New Testament Greek Lexicon" 1999, www.biblestudytools.com

COMMON TERMS

The words *children, child,* and *offspring* are used interchangeably, but it will be more effective to insert the specific names of the child, children, or group of young people being prayed for.

Day 1

I REPENT

---

1. Dear Lord I repent for forgetting that as a parent I am only a custodian/guardian of your children and that it is a great privilege.

   Lo, children are an heritage of the Lord:
   and the fruit of the womb is his reward.
   (Psalm 127:3 KJV)

2. Father please forgive me for mothering in my own strength and trying to control my children's destiny.

   Just as you cannot understand the path of the wind or the mystery of a tiny baby growing in its mother's womb, so you cannot understand the activity of God, who does all things.
   (Ecclesiastes 11:5 NLT)

3. I repent for worrying and being anxious about my children. Lord help me to obey your word and begin to pray and present my requests to you.

> Do not be anxious about anything, but in every situation, by prayer and petition, with thanksgiving, present your requests to God. (Philippians 4:6 NIV)

4. O God I know that I am guilty of sin. Lord I repent, please have mercy on me. By reason of the cross and blood of Jesus let not the mistakes I have made affect my children negatively.

> I lavish unfailing love to a thousand generations. I forgive iniquity, rebellion, and sin. But I do not excuse the guilty. I lay the sins of the parents upon their children and grandchildren; the entire family is affected—even children in the third and fourth generations. (Exodus 34:7 NLT)

Day 2

CHILD, YOU WILL MAKE HEAVEN

1. My children (*insert names*) will not depart from the Christian values and training I instilled in them.

   Train up a child in the way he should go: and when he is old, he will not depart from it. (Proverbs 22:6 KJV)

2. I declare that my children will keep the way of the Lord and do what is right and just.

   For I know him, that he will command his children and his household after him, and they shall keep the way of the Lord, to do justice and judgment; that the Lord may bring upon Abraham that which he hath spoken of him. (Genesis 18:19 KJV)

3. My entire household shall be saved; I pray all my children and grandchildren will make heaven because I believe in Jesus, and I am born again.

> And they said, Believe on the Lord Jesus
> Christ, and thou shalt be saved, and thy
> house. (Acts 16:31 KJV)

4. Lord, fight those who fight me and are trying to
capture my children. Lord, save my children; save
my children.

> But thus saith the Lord, Even the captives
> of the mighty shall be taken away, and the
> prey of the terrible shall be delivered: for
> I will contend with him that contendeth
> with thee, and I will save thy children.
> (Isaiah 49:25 KJV)

5. I refuse to shed any more tears; my prodigal children
must return. I do not care how far they have gone.
There is hope they are coming home to me.

> But now this is what the Lord says: "Do
> not weep any longer, for I will reward
> you," says the Lord. "Your children will
> come back to you from the distant land of
> the enemy. There is hope for your future,"
> says the Lord. "Your children will come
> again to their own land. But now this is
> what the Lord says: "Do not weep any
> longer, for I will reward you," says the
> Lord. "Your children will come back to

you from the distant land of the enemy. There is hope for your future," says the Lord. "Your children will come again to their own land." (Jeremiah 31:16–17 NLT)

Day 3

RIGHTEOUS COMPANY

1. Lord, keep my son/daughter away from those who will seduce and entice him/her. Expose the ambushes set for my child, and empower him/her to resist the devil and his temptations.

   My son, if sinners entice thee, consent thou not. If they say, Come with us, let us lay wait for blood, let us lurk privily for the innocent without cause: (Proverbs 1:10–11 KJV)

2. (Insert child's name), you shall not fall into the snare of angry and hot-tempered people. Do not imbibe their ways and corrupt your spirit. May the peace and joy of the Lord reign in your heart.

   Do not associate with a man given to anger; Or go with a hot-tempered man, Or you will learn his ways And find a snare for yourself. (Proverbs 22:24 NASB)

3. Child, you are too blessed. You will not walk in the counsel of the wicked, stand in the path of sinners, or hang around mean people.

   Blessed is the man that walketh not in the counsel of the ungodly, nor standeth in the way of sinners, nor sitteth in the seat of the scornful. But his delight is in the law of the Lord; and in his law doth he meditate day and night. (Psalm 1:1–2 KJV)

4. I terminate any and every relationship you have with bad company in Jesus's name. I break every unholy alliance; you shall not be corrupted.

   Be not deceived: evil communications corrupt good manners.
   (1 Corinthians 15:33 KJV)

5. I pray (Insert child's name), you will always be surrounded by wise people and wise counsel, in school, at work, or wherever you find yourself, so you will not suffer harm.

   He that walketh with wise men shall be wise: but a companion of fools shall be destroyed. (Proverbs 13:20 KJV)

6. I dissociate (insert child's name) from immorality, covetousness, idolatry, and drunkenness, and those who engage in such practices.

> But now I have written unto you not to keep company, if any man that is called a brother be a fornicator, or covetous, or an idolator, or a railer, or a drunkard, or an extortioner; with such an one no not to eat. (1 Corinthians 5:11 KJV)

Day 4

STEPS ORDERED BY GOD

1. O God, order my children's steps. Keep them from losing their way.

   > The steps of a good man are ordered by the Lord: and he delighteth in his way. (Psalm 37:23 KJV)

2. Lord, show my children the way they should go. They think they know, but they do not. Help them to follow your leading.

   > A person's steps are directed by the LORD. How then can anyone understand their own way? (Proverbs 20:24 NIV)

3. Jehovah, make their path perfect; make them walk in the excellent way.

   > It is God that girdeth me with strength, and maketh my way perfect. (Psalm 18:32 KJV)

4. Make a way for my children, even in the dry seasons of their lives. Make a way, Lord, when there seems to be no way.

   > I will even make a way in the wilderness, and rivers in the desert. (Isaiah 43:19b KJV)

5. Spirit of God, lead my children on level ground. Go before them, and make the crooked places straight.

   > Teach me to do Your will, For You are my God; Let Your good Spirit lead me on level ground. (Psalm 143:10 NASB)

6. Father, please make my children live according to your word and to really enjoy it.

   > Make me to go in the path of thy commandments; for therein do I delight. (Psalm 119:35 KJV)

7. Let the light and truth of God lead my children to abide in his presence always.

   > O send out thy light and thy truth: let them lead me; let them bring me unto thy holy hill, and to thy tabernacles. (Psalm 43:3 KJV)

Day 5

SPIRIT OF EXCELLENCE

1. You (insert child's name) will excel in everything
   you do; may God also grant you the grace to excel
   in giving to the service of God.

   > Therefore, as ye abound in everything,
   > in faith, and utterance, and knowledge,
   > and in all diligence, and in your love to
   > us, see that ye abound in this grace also.
   > (2 Corinthians 8:7 KJV)

2. Do everything with all your might: school, work,
   business, and ministry. (Child's name), put your all
   into everything do. God help him/her.

   > Whatsoever thy hand findeth to do, do it
   > with thy might. (Ecclesiastes 9:10a KJV)

3. Lord, give my children exceptional abilities that
   they may be distinguished among their peers in
   Jesus's name.

   > Now Daniel so distinguished himself
   > among the administrators and the

satraps by his exceptional qualities that the king planned to set him over the whole kingdom. (Daniel 6:3 NIV)

4. Father, give my children spiritual understanding and an excellent spirit. The spirit of foolishness will not influence my children.

He that hath knowledge spareth his words: [and] a man of understanding is of an excellent spirit. (Proverbs 17:27 KJV)

5. May a spirit of excellence be found in (child's name) so that he/she becomes a problem solver in this generation.

Forasmuch as an excellent spirit, and knowledge, and understanding, interpreting of dreams, and shewing of hard sentences, and dissolving of doubts, were found in the same Daniel, whom the king named Belteshazzar: now let Daniel be called, and he will shew the interpretation. (Daniel 5:12 KJV)

6. My children shall be examples of good works, integrity, and dignity in Jesus's name. I pray no one will be able to speak evil of you.

In all things shewing thyself a pattern of good works: in doctrine shewing uncorruptness, gravity, sincerity, sound speech, that he that cannot be condemned; that he that is of contrary part may be ashamed, having no evil to say of you. (Titus 2:7 KJV)

Day 6

CALL TO PURPOSE

1. My children are called out of darkness into God's wonderful light. They are specially chosen by God and will fulfill their destinies in Christ.

> But ye are a chosen generation, a royal priesthood, an holy nation, a peculiar people; that ye should shew forth the praises of him who hath called you out of darkness into his marvellous light.
> (1 Peter 2:9 KJV)

2. My children are called to a life of righteousness and holiness for God's glory. Lord, be glorified in their daily lives. Enable them with your grace.

> Who hath saved us, and called us with an holy calling, not according to our works, but according to his own purpose and grace, which was given us in Christ Jesus before the world began.
> (2 Timothy 1:9 KJV)

3. My children are called to freedom from sickness, iniquity, fear, bondage, and curses. They cannot be entangled again; they are totally free in Jesus's name.

    > You, my brothers and sisters, were called to be free. But do not use your freedom to indulge the flesh[a]; rather, serve one another humbly in love. (Galatians 5:13 NIV)

4. I declare my children's hearts will be enlightened so that they know the hope of their calling in Christ and walk in it.

    > The eyes of your understanding being enlightened; that ye may know what is the hope of his calling, and what the riches of the glory of his inheritance in the saints. (Ephesians 1:18 KJV)

5. Lord, be with my son/daughter. Let his or her name be known in the nations. Let his or her fame precede him or her to the glory of your name.

    > So the Lord was with Joshua, and his fame was in all the land. (Joshua 6:2 AMP)

6. Jehovah, cause all things to work together for good for my children. Let it work in their favor to fulfill purpose in their lives.

> And we know that all things work together for good to them that love God, to them who are the called according to his purpose. (Romans 8:28 KJV)

Day 7

YOU WILL FLOURISH

1. Son/daughter, wealth and riches shall be in your house, and God's righteousness will reign in your life in Jesus name.

   Wealth and riches shall be in his house: and his righteousness endureth for ever. (Psalm 112:3 KJV)

2. May the Lord give you power to make wealth and be successful in all you do.

   Remember the Lord your God. He is the one who gives you power to be successful, in order to fulfill the covenant he confirmed to your ancestors with an oath. (Deuteronomy 8:18 NLT)

3. Child, God will promote you and set you up. He will make way for you. Even when you are not qualified, God will override the rules and others and promote you.

> For promotion cometh neither from the east, nor from the west, nor from the south. But God is the judge: he putteth down one, and setteth up another. (Psalm 75:6–7 KJV)

4. I pray that my children will meditate on God's word and live accordingly; they shall be prosperous and successful.

> This book of the law shall not depart out of thy mouth; but thou shalt meditate therein day and night, that thou mayest observe to do according to all that is written therein: for then thou shalt make thy way prosperous, and then thou shalt have good success. (Joshua 1:8 KJV)

5. My sons/daughters are rooted and grounded in the house of the Lord and are flourishing spiritually, emotionally, mentally, and physically. Their families are flourishing; their careers are flourishing. God is glorified in their lives.

> The righteous shall flourish like the palm tree: he shall grow like a cedar in Lebanon. Those that be planted in the house of the Lord shall flourish in the courts of our God. (Psalm 92:12–13 KJV)

6. O Lord, open the heavens over my children and pour out buckets of your goodness upon them in Jesus's name. Flood their lives with your amazing blessings of righteousness, peace, and joy.

Open up, heavens, and rain. Clouds, pour out buckets of my goodness! (Isaiah 45:8 MSG)

Day 8

GOD WILL ESTABLISH

1. God has established my son/daughter in his/her calling, and the enemy cannot do anything about it

   And all Israel from Dan even to Beersheba knew that Samuel was established to be a prophet of the Lord. (1 Samuel 3:20 KJV)

2. God's covenant is established with my seed and their seed in Jesus's name—covenants of blessing, righteousness, increase, healing, and salvation.

   And I, behold, I establish my covenant with you, and with your seed after you. (Genesis 9:9 KJV)

3. My children shall obey God's commands and walk in his ways, and the Lord will establish them in all they do.

   The Lord shall establish thee an holy people unto himself, as he hath sworn unto thee, if thou shalt keep the commandments of

the Lord thy God, and walk in his ways.
(Deuteronomy 28:9 KJV)

4. I commit the works of my children unto the Lord;
   O God, establish their plans.

   Commit thy works unto the Lord,
   and thy thoughts shall be established.
   (Proverbs 16:3 KJV)

5. Lord, cause my children to be accomplished in the
   nations, and grant them peace in their hearts and
   minds.

   Lord, you establish peace for us; all that
   we have accomplished you have done for
   us. (Isaiah 26:12 NIV)

6. Father, I will give you no rest until I see my
   offspring established as the praise of the earth.
   Lord lift (insert child's name) up and make his/her
   life praiseworthy.

   And give him no rest, till he establish,
   and till he make Jerusalem a praise in the
   earth. (Isaiah 62:7 KJV)

7. Prosper my children and establish them in life;
   punish anyone who oppresses them.

> Their children also shall be as aforetime, and their congregation shall be established before me, and I will punish all that oppress them. (Jeremiah 30:20 KJV)

8. I pray my children are rooted and grounded in love of God and Christ dwells deeply in their hearts.

   > That Christ may dwell in your hearts by faith; that ye, being rooted and grounded in love. (Ephesians 3:17 KJV)

9. My children will never be uprooted from their place of honor; no one can remove them or take their place.

   > The righteous will never be uprooted, but the wicked will not remain in the land. (Proverbs 10:30 NIV)

10. Establish the steps of my children (insert names), O Lord, regardless of whatever they have conjured in their minds or hearts.

    > A man's heart deviseth his way: but the Lord directeth his steps. (Proverbs 16:9 KJV)

Day 9

EXPECTED END—DESTINY

1. My children will fulfill their God-given destiny in Jesus's name; they will arrive at their expected end.

   > For I know the thoughts that I think toward you, saith the Lord, thoughts of peace, and not of evil, to give you an expected end. (Jeremiah 29:11 KJV)

2. O Lord, do for my (insert name of your child) whatsoever you have planned; whatever it takes, let only your will be done in their lives.

   > For he performeth the thing that is appointed for me: and many such things are with him. (Job 23:14 KJV)

3. O Lord, guide them with your wise counsel, and lead them to a glorious destiny.

   > Thou shalt guide me with thy counsel, and afterward receive me to glory. (Psalm 73:24 KJV)

4. Whatsoever is resisting my son's/daughter's already decided destiny, I come against you now and release him or her into everything God has called him or her to.

> Everything has already been decided. It was known long ago what each person would be. So there's no use arguing with God about your destiny. (Ecclesiastes 6:10 NLT)

5. Son/daughter you have been set apart, you have been called even before you were born, and you shall impact your generation for God.

> Before I formed thee in the belly I knew thee; and before thou camest forth out of the womb I sanctified thee, and I ordained thee a prophet unto the nations. (Jeremiah 1:5 KJV)

6. My children's records shall be flawless because God almighty is with them.

> Samuel grew up. God was with him, and Samuel's prophetic record was flawless. (1 Samuel 3:19 MSG)

7. Lord please instruct my children on how to make their life choices that they might fulfill their destiny in you.

What man is he that feareth the Lord? him shall he teach in the way that he shall choose. (Psalm 25:12 KJV)

Day 10

A SOUND MIND

1. Son/daughter, you do not have a spirit of timidity or cowardice. You have a spirit of power and sound judgment. You are disciplined and well balanced and have self-control.

   > For God did not give us a spirit of timidity or cowardice or fear, but [He has given us a spirit] of power and of love and of sound judgment and personal discipline [abilities that result in a calm, well-balanced mind and self-control].
   > (2 Timothy 1:7 AMP)

2. Son/daughter, you shall walk humbly before God. I declare that you are wise and have a sound mind. Therefore, you make correct decisions that will cause you to advance in life.

   > But with the humble [the teachable who have been chiseled by trial and who have learned to walk humbly with God]

there is wisdom and soundness of mind. (Proverbs 11:2 AMP)

3. A perverse mind is not your portion. You will not engage in things that will attract contempt. May God give you great insight and foresight that will take you to the place of honor.

   A man will be commended according to his insight and sound judgment, But the one who is of a perverse mind will be despised. (Proverbs 12:8 KJV)

4. I declare that my children shall stay focused on the things of God in these last days and will be sober and watchful in prayer.

   But the end of all things is at hand: be ye therefore sober, and watch unto prayer. (1 Peter 4:7 KJV)

5. I reject every plan of the enemy to make my children lose their mind. I take authority over mental health issues—depression, anxiety, bipolar disorder, schizophrenia. It is not your portion. You have a sound mind!

But he said, I am not mad, most noble Festus; but speak forth the words of truth and soberness. (Acts 26:25 KJV)

6. Children, center your mind on and implant in your heart only the things that are pure, honorable, right, and confirmed by God's word.

> Finally, brethren, whatsoever things are true, whatsoever things are honest, whatsoever things are just, whatsoever things are pure, whatsoever things are lovely, whatsoever things are of good report; if there be any virtue, and if there be any praise, think on these things. (Philippians 4:8 KJV)

7. I destroy every proud obstacle that keeps my children from knowing or growing in Christ. I capture every rebellious thought and subject them to the obedience of Christ.

> Casting down imaginations, and every high thing that exalteth itself against the knowledge of God, and bringing into captivity every thought to the obedience of Christ. (2 Corinthians 10:5 KJV)

Day 11

ANOINTING

1. O God, honor my offspring and anoint them with oil. Cause their cups to overflow as their enemies look on but cannot touch them.

   Thou preparest a table before me in the presence of mine enemies: thou anointest my head with oil; my cup runneth over. (Psalm 23:5 KJV)

2. May the anointing teach my children and my grandchildren about all things and in every situation they find themselves. Keep them in your will dear Father.

   But as the same anointing teacheth you of all things, and is truth, and is no lie, and even as it hath taught you, ye shall abide in him. (1 John 2:27b KJV)

3. Lord God, set my son/daughter above all his or her contemporaries by anointing him or her with oil of joy.

> Thou lovest righteousness, and hatest wickedness: therefore God, thy God, hath anointed thee with the oil of gladness above thy fellows. (Psalm 45:7 KJV)

4. Satan, you dare not touch my anointed children and cannot harm them. They are off limits in Jesus's name.

> Saying, Touch not mine anointed, and do my prophets no harm. (Psalm 105:15 KJV)

5. Lord, by your anointing upon my children, you will empower them to subdue nations, and their kings will submit to them. Yes, doors of opportunity will open for them that can never be shut again.

> Thus saith the Lord to his anointed, to Cyrus, whose right hand I have holden, to subdue nations before him; and I will loose the loins of kings, to open before him the two leaved gates; and the gates shall not be shut. (Isaiah 45:1 KJV)

6. [Insert name of son/daughter], the Spirit of God is upon you because God has anointed you to share the gospel and be used by him to touch your generation. Your voice will be heard, and God will be glorified through your life.

The Spirit of the Lord God is upon me; because the Lord hath anointed me to preach good tidings unto the meek; he hath sent me to bind up the brokenhearted, to proclaim liberty to the captives, and the opening of the prison to them that are bound. (Isaiah 61:1 NIV)

7. Son/daughter, God has anointed you with excellence and grace, and you are blessed forever.

Thou art fairer than the children of men: grace is poured into thy lips: therefore God hath blessed thee for ever. (Psalm 45:2 KJV)

Day 12

BONE OF MY BONES

1. My son/daughter will not marry outside God's will. He or she will find the bone of his or her bones, yes, the flesh of his or her flesh—the one God has prepared for him or her.

   And Adam said, This is now bone of my bones, and flesh of my flesh: she shall be called Woman, because she was taken out of Man. (Genesis 2:23 KJV)

2. My son's wife/daughter's husband shall have a principled character. She/he will be a blessing and my son/daughter will trust her/him fully.

   Who can find a virtuous woman? for her price is far above rubies. The heart of her husband doth safely trust in her, so that he shall have no need of spoil. She will do him good and not evil all the days of her life. (Proverbs 31:10–12 KJV)

3. I pray that my children's marriages are blessed beyond measure and full of joy and rejoicing.

> Let thy fountain be blessed: and rejoice with the wife of thy youth. (Proverbs 5:18 KJV)

4. May my son find a true and faithful wife, a good wife, and my daughter be found by a godly man approved by God.

> He who finds a [true and faithful] wife finds a good thing And obtains favor and approval from the Lord. (Proverbs 18:22 AMP)

5. My children's spouses are wise, understanding, and sensible—real gifts from God.

> House and wealth are the inheritance from fathers, But a wise, understanding, and sensible wife is [a gift and blessing] from the Lord. (Proverbs 19:14 AMP)

6. I take authority over any adulterous spirit attacking my children's marriages in Jesus's name. I plead the blood of Jesus over their union. I declare their marital bed undefiled.

So he that goeth in to his neighbour's wife; whosoever toucheth her shall not be innocent. (Proverbs 6:29 KJV)

7. Lord lead my son/daughter to his or her ordained spouse. Keep him or her from making a mistake.

> And he said, Blessed be the Lord God of my master Abraham, who hath not left destitute my master of his mercy and his truth: I being in the way, the Lord led me to the house of my master's brethren. (Genesis 24:27 KJV)

8. Divorce is not my children's portion; I reject it in Jesus's name. Lord, please keep their marriage until death. I speak health and wealth into their holy union. Help them through their challenges.

> And unto the married I command, yet not I, but the Lord, Let not the wife depart from her husband. (1 Corinthians 7:10 KJV)

9. I pray for mutual love, respect, and understanding for my children and their spouses. God, grant them the grace to live according to knowledge of one another, that their prayers be not hindered.

> Likewise, ye wives, be in subjection to your own husbands; that, if any obey not the word, they also may without the word be won by the conversation of the wives … Likewise, ye husbands, dwell with them according to knowledge, giving honor unto the wife, as unto the weaker vessel, and as being heirs together of the grace of life; that your prayers be not hindered. (1 Peter 3:1,7 KJV)

10. Keep my children holy, O Lord, especially in marriage, that they may not fall into sexual sin and lust that leads to adultery. I pray for them to have control over their bodies and to live holy lives.

> God's will is for you to be holy, so stay away from all sexual sin. Then each of you will control his own body[a] and live in holiness and honor—not in lustful passion like the pagans who do not know God and his ways. (1 Thessalonians 4:3–5 NLT)

11. May [insert your child's name] spouse be a good and uplifting communicator. Lord, keep their marriage from malice, filthy language, and anger.

> But now ye also put off all these; anger, wrath, malice, blasphemy, filthy

communication out of your mouth. (Colossians 3:8 KJV)

12. Lord, make my child's spouse a man/woman after God's own heart, a maturing Christian who can play a spiritual role that encourages my son/daughter toward deeper spiritual growth.

Husbands, love your wives, even as Christ also loved the church, and gave himself for it. (Ephesians 5:25 KJV)

Day 13

ACADEMICS, JOB,
AND CAREER

---

1. Son/daughter, you are the head and not the tail. In everything you do in your education or in your career, you will come out on top. I reject a losing or failure mind-set. You are above and not beneath. You have the spirit of an accomplisher, yes, the spirit of a champion.

   > And the Lord shall make thee the head, and not the tail; and thou shalt be above only, and thou shalt not be beneath; if that thou hearken unto the commandments of the Lord thy God, which I command thee this day, to observe and to do them. (Deuteronomy 28:13 KJV)

2. God, distinguish my offspring as you did Daniel. Set them above even their teachers, bosses, and contemporaries. I decree that their exceptional gifts will position them in high places.

> Then this Daniel was preferred above the presidents and princes, because an excellent spirit was in him; and the king thought to set him over the whole realm. (Daniel 6:3 KJV)

3. An excellent spirit will be found in my son/daughter. O Lord, please give him or her incredible knowledge and wisdom to bring solution to any problem he or she is confronted with—in Jesus's name. Every anti-excellence demon reinforcing against my children, be bound in the name of Jesus.

> Forasmuch as an excellent spirit, and knowledge, and understanding, interpreting of dreams, and shewing of hard sentences, and dissolving of doubts, were found in the same Daniel, whom the king named Belteshazzar: now let Daniel be called, and he will shew the interpretation. (Daniel 5:12 KJV)

4. My children's acumen surpasses even their teachers because of the power of the rhema word in their spirits. Keep them meditating on your word, O Lord.

I have more understanding than all my teachers: for thy testimonies are my meditation. (Psalm 119:99 KJV)

5. My children live above the anti-Christ instructions, values, and influences of the world today because they are imparted and influenced by Jehovah God. Great is their peace!

   And all thy children shall be taught of the Lord; and great shall be the peace of thy children. (Isaiah 54:13 KJV)

6. Covenant-keeping God, give my son/daughter the power to succeed in all he or she does. Fulfill your promise, O God, and cause them to succeed.

   Remember the Lord your God. He is the one who gives you power to be successful, in order to fulfill the covenant he confirmed to your ancestors with an oath. (Deuteronomy 8:18 NLT)

7. Lord, give my children a spirit of knowledge, wisdom, and unusual aptitude for understanding that will place them at the top as you did for the four Hebrew children.

As for these four children, God gave them knowledge and skill in all learning and wisdom: and Daniel had understanding in all visions and dreams. (Daniel 1:17 KJV)

Day 14

POWER TO MAKE WEALTH

1. O God, give my children the knowhow and the help
   they need to produce not just riches but incredible
   wealth. Lord, teach them, help them. Provide divine
   avenues and networks for wealth to come forth in
   their lives, that they will be your vessels of blessing
   in the kingdom.

   > But remember the Lord your God, for it
   > is he who gives you the ability to produce
   > wealth, and so confirms his covenant,
   > which he swore to your ancestors, as it is
   > today. (Deuteronomy 8:18 NIV)

2. Whatsoever my children do will surely prosper
   because they are positioned and rooted like trees
   by rivers of water, so they produce in the God-
   ordained seasons of their lives.

   > And he shall be like a tree planted by the
   > rivers of water, that bringeth forth his
   > fruit in his season; his leaf also shall not

wither; and whatsoever he doeth shall prosper. (Psalm 1:3 KJV)

3. I call forth testimonies of the Lord as He delightfully prospers my children continuously— more testimonies, Lord, more.

   Let them shout for joy, and be glad, that favor my righteous cause: yea, let them say continually, Let the Lord be magnified, which hath pleasure in the prosperity of his servant. (Psalm 35:27 KJV)

4. Jehovah Jireh, fill my children's barns until full and overflowing; let them lack nothing. Supply all their needs according to your riches in glory.

   But my God shall supply all your need according to his riches in glory by Christ Jesus. (Philippians 4:19 KJV)

5. Thank you for blessing my children: thank you for blessing of life, the blessing of health, the blessing of the fruit of the womb, the blessing of peace and joy. You call them blessed and add no sorrow.

   The blessing of the Lord, it maketh rich, and he addeth no sorrow with it. (Proverbs 10:22 KJV)

6. Lord, it is your desire that all my children succeed and be healthy. Heal them, Lord. Help them, Lord, to succeed.

> Beloved, I wish above all things that thou mayest prosper and be in health, even as thy soul prospereth. (3 John 2 KJV)

7. Make my children prosper, make them succeed, make them flourish, and make them grow. Make them advance, make them productive, make them increase, and make them rise.

> I, even I, have spoken; yea, I have called him: I have brought him, and he shall make his way prosperous. (Isaiah 48:15 KJV)

8. My son/daughter's special gifts and talents will be instruments of blessing to all, which will prosper whenever or wherever they are activated.

> A gift is as a precious stone in the eyes of him that hath it: whithersoever it turneth, it prospereth. (Proverbs 17:8 KJV)

9. Father, please deliver my children from financial troubles. Do not leave them struggling, give them financial freedom. Make their treasuries full.

Save now, I beseech thee, O Lord: O Lord,
I beseech thee, send now prosperity.
(Psalm 118:25 KJV)

10. My son/ daughter will prosper in all his/her works.
Everything he or she engages in will prosper to the
glory of the Lord.

And Hezekiah prospered in all his works.
(2 Chronicles 32:30b KJV)

Day 15

FREEDOM FROM STRONGHOLDS

1. I take authority over every stronghold in my children's lives, and I plead the blood of Jesus over them and destroy every satanic grip and false argument by the power of God

   > The weapons we use in our fight are not the world's weapons but God's powerful weapons, which we use to destroy strongholds. We destroy false arguments. (2 Corinthians 10:4 GN)

2. Lord, please destroy the work and influence of every demon that plagues my son and daughter from the root in Jesus's name.

   > That strengtheneth the spoiled against the strong, so that the spoiled shall come against the fortress. (Amos 5:9 KJV)

3. Dear Father, cleanse my children from any sin lurking in their hearts, especially those hidden sins

that easily beset them. I declare, son/daughter, that you have the power to resist temptation in Jesus's name. I plead the blood of Jesus over you.

> How can I know all the sins lurking in my heart? Cleanse me from these hidden faults. (Psalm 19:12 NLT)

4. I bind every demonic activity in the lives of my children and loose God's freedom, peace, joy, love, strength, and blessings in their lives in the mighty name of Jesus.

> And I will give unto thee the keys of the kingdom of heaven: and whatsoever thou shalt bind on earth shall be bound in heaven: and whatsoever thou shalt loose on earth shall be loosed in heaven. (Matthew 16:19 KJV)

5. Fight for my children, O Lord, and do not let the evil one go unpunished. Free my children indeed. Free to serve and worship you.

> Though hand join in hand, the wicked shall not be unpunished: but the seed of the righteous shall be delivered. (Proverbs 11:21 KJV)

6. Son/daughter, I pray that you submit to the authority of God so you will stand firmly against the devil and his cohorts.

> Submit yourselves therefore to God. Resist the devil, and he will flee from you. (James 4:7 KJV)

7. God's word does not return to him void. It must accomplish that which it is sent to do, so son/daughter, may every word of God that has been prayed or spoken to you fulfill its purpose in your life.

> For the word of God is quick, and powerful, and sharper than any two edged sword, piercing even to the dividing asunder of soul and spirit, and of the joints and marrow, and is a discerner of the thoughts and intents of the heart. (Hebrews 4:12 KJV)

8. Satan, you cannot devour any of my offspring for you will not find them on your journey of destruction for they are hidden in the palm of the Lord.

> Be sober, be vigilant; because your adversary the devil, as a roaring lion,

walketh about, seeking whom he may devour. (1 Peter 5:8 KJV)

9. Glory be to God. Jehovah, the man of war, the stronger one, has overpowered Satan in the lives of my children. By his finger he has driven out the demons. I take back all that the devil has stolen from my children in Jesus's name.

> But if I with the finger of God cast out devils, no doubt the kingdom of God is come upon you. When a strong man armed keepeth his palace, his goods are in peace. (Luke 11:20–22 KJV)

Day 16

SICKNESS AND DISEASE

1. Jesus! Jesus! Your name still heals today. You heal any and every manner of sickness and disease. Cancer must go, sickle cell disease must go, mental health issues must go, autoimmune diseases must go. Every manner of disease you must go. My children are healed in Jesus's name.

> And Jesus went about all Galilee, teaching in their synagogues, and preaching the gospel of the kingdom, and healing all manner of sickness and all manner of disease among the people. (Matthew 4:23 KJV)

2. I reject every attack of illness upon my offspring; remain in hell, where you belong. In Jesus's name!

> And the Lord will take away from thee all sickness, and will put none of the evil diseases of Egypt, which thou knowest, upon thee; but will lay them upon all them that hate thee. (Deuteronomy 7:15 KJV)

3. O Lord, indeed there is nothing too difficult for you. Regardless of what the doctors have said, I know that my son/daughter is healed and whole.

> Behold, I am the Lord, the God of all flesh: is there anything too hard for me? (Jeremiah 32:27 KJV)

4. I loose God's healing power upon my children and bind every sickness and disease that dares to attack them. I plead the blood of Jesus over them.

> Verily I say unto you, Whatsoever ye shall bind on earth shall be bound in heaven: and whatsoever ye shall loose on earth shall be loosed in heaven. (Matthew 18:18 KJV)

5. I declare the manifestation of the finished work of the cross in the life of my son/daughter. By the stripes of Jesus Christ, they are healed.

> But he was wounded for our transgressions, he was bruised for our iniquities: the chastisement of our peace was upon him; and with his stripes we are healed. (Isaiah 53:5 KJV)

6. Father, let your resurrection power quicken my son/daughter's body and mind. Give life to those things that seem dead or dying in the mighty name of Jesus.

> But if the Spirit of him that raised up Jesus from the dead dwell in you, he that raised up Christ from the dead shall also quicken your mortal bodies by his Spirit that dwelleth in you. (Romans 8:11 KJV)

7. In the authority of Christ, I cast out every demonic ailment or spirit of infirmity that is plaguing my son/daughter in Jesus's name. I plead the blood of Jesus, and I command total healing.

> And when he had called unto him his twelve disciples, he gave them power against unclean spirits, to cast them out, and to heal all manner of sickness and all manner of disease. (Matthew 10:1 KJV)

8. By faith I anoint you (son/daughter) with oil to be healed and strong again. You are well in Jesus's name.

> Is any sick among you? let him call for the elders of the church; and let them pray over him, anointing him with oil

in the name of the Lord: And the prayer
of faith shall save the sick, and the
Lord shall raise him up; and if he have
committed sins, they shall be forgiven
him. (James 5:14–15 KJV)

9. My children will not grow weary in Jesus's name.
They were born to soar, so they will mount up like
eagles and soar, to the glory of the Lord.

But they that wait upon the Lord shall
renew their strength; they shall mount up
with wings as eagles; they shall run, and
not be weary; and they shall walk, and
not faint. (Isaiah 40:31 KJV)

10. Restore my son/daughter's health, O Lord. Heal
his or her mental, physical, spiritual, or emotional
wounds. Let the balm of Gilead make him or her
whole.

For I will restore health unto thee, and
I will heal thee of thy wounds, saith
the Lord; because they called thee an
Outcast, saying, This is Zion, whom no
man seeketh after. (Jeremiah 30:17 KJV)

11. Father, I stand in the gap and ask for forgiveness for my children's sins. Have mercy on them and heal them, O God.

> Bless the Lord, O my soul, and forget not all his benefits: Who forgiveth all thine iniquities; who healeth all thy diseases. (Psalm 103:2–3 KJV)

Day 17

No Weapon Shall Prosper

1. [Insert son's/daughter's name], nothing the enemy can plot against you can prosper. I refute the negative things being said about you, your soul, your health, your marriage, your education, your career, your finances, and your future. My children shall triumph over opposition, and God almighty vindicate them.

   > No weapon that is formed against thee shall prosper; and every tongue that shall rise against thee in judgment thou shalt condemn. This is the heritage of the servants of the Lord, and their righteousness is of me, saith the Lord. (Isaiah 54:17 KJV)

2. I stand still and watch my God, the man of war, fight for my children. Lord, the battle belongs to you, and I know that I know that my children have the victory in Jesus's name.

The Lord shall fight for you, and ye shall
hold your peace. (Exodus 14:14 KJV)

3. O Lord, smite the enemy of my offspring, and cause
all that come against them to flee in seven ways.
Destroy every satanic assignment against them, in
Jesus's name.

The Lord shall cause thine enemies that
rise up against thee to be smitten before
thy face: they shall come out against thee
one way, and flee before thee seven ways.
(Deuteronomy 28:7 KJV)

4. Lord, you are a man of war, Yahweh is your name.
Strengthen my children; do not allow them to be
weary. Humiliate the enemy before them.

For thou hast girded me with strength
unto the battle: thou hast subdued
under me those that rose up against me.
(Psalm 18:39 KJV)

5. Deliver my children, Lord, from all who come
against them. I declare that regardless of the battle,
they will come through unscathed.

He rescues me unharmed from the battle waged against me, even though many oppose me. (Psalm 55:18 NIV)

6. I command you evildoers to wither away in Jesus's name! Stop parading in my children's lives like the angel of light; be exposed for who you really are.

Fret not thyself because of evildoers, neither be thou envious against the workers of iniquity. For they shall soon be cut down like the grass, and wither as the green herb. (Psalm 37:1–2 KJV)

7. O Lord keep (insert child's name) as the apple of your eye. Hide him/her from the wicked who seek to destroy him/her.

Keep me as the apple of the eye, hide me under the shadow of thy wings, From the wicked that oppress me, from my deadly enemies, who compass me about. (Psalm 17:8–9 KJV)

Day 18

DESTROY THE INFLUENCE OF MOLECH, JEZEBEL, AND DELILAH

1. My seed or offspring shall never ever be sacrificed to Molech (an ancient god that demanded children be sacrificed to it). My children will live and not die a sudden or unnecessary death, but they will live to fulfil their destiny in Christ.

> Again, thou shalt say to the children of Israel, Whosoever he be of the children of Israel, or of the strangers that sojourn in Israel, that giveth any of his seed unto Molech; he shall surely be put to death: the people of the land shall stone him with stones. And I will set my face against that man, and will cut him off from among his people; because he hath given of his seed unto Molech, to defile my sanctuary, and to profane my holy name. (Leviticus 20:2–3 KJV)

2. I plead the blood of Jesus over my children and put a hedge of fire round about them, that the spirit of Jezebel will never find them in her quest to kill, but she will be destroyed and her influence over them broken.

   And the dogs shall eat Jezebel in the portion of Jezreel, and there shall be none to bury her. And he opened the door, and fled. (2 Kings 9:10 KJV)

3. None of my children will fall into the deep pit or evil affections of strange women or men in the name of Jesus. I expose their schemes and destroy any influence on my children by the blood of Jesus.

   The mouth of strange women is a deep pit: he that is abhorred of the Lord shall fall therein. (Proverbs 22:14 KJV)

4. I take authority over the spirit of Delilah; you will not seduce my son/daughter into relinquishing their power and anointing. Lord, strengthen them, keep them from falling into Delilah's trap.

   And Samson called unto the Lord, and said, O Lord God, remember me, I pray thee, and strengthen me, I pray thee, only this once, O God, that I may be at once avenged of the Philistines for my two eyes. (Judges 16:28 KJV)

5. All you demons assigned to dig pits for my children fall into your own pit. You who have broken the walls attempting to gain access into any of my children's lives will be bitten by the snake yourself. I protect my children by a hedge of fire and the blood of Jesus; no demon can penetrate in Jesus's name.

He that diggeth a pit shall fall into it; and whoso breaketh an hedge, a serpent shall bite him. (Ecclesiastes 10:8 KJV)

Day 19

SPIRITUAL ALIGNMENT

1. My son/daughter will not be tossed to and fro by the deceptive teaching of today. He/she will not buy into Satan's lies and tricks. He/she will be mature and sound in the things of God.

   > That we henceforth be no more children, tossed to and fro, and carried about with every wind of doctrine, by the sleight of men, and cunning craftiness, whereby they lie in wait to deceive. (Ephesians 4:14 KJV)

2. My children will not be conformed to the world's standards, but I pray for their minds to be renewed and transformed so they are not deceived but will follow only the will of God.

   > And be not conformed to this world: but be ye transformed by the renewing of your mind, that ye may prove what is that good, and acceptable, and perfect, will of God. (Romans 12:2 KJV)

3. I pray my children will not be double-minded and
   that they will be faithfully committed to God.
   Draw them close to you, Lord.

   > Draw nigh to God, and he will draw nigh
   > to you. Cleanse your hands, ye sinners;
   > and purify your hearts, ye double minded.
   > (James 4:8 KJV)

4. Son/daughter, you will not keep the company
   of ungodly friends and sinners or embrace the
   mockers or scornful people. In Jesus's name, you
   will take pleasure in Christ and obey the word
   of God.

   > Blessed is the man that walketh not in the
   > counsel of the ungodly, nor standeth in
   > the way of sinners, nor sitteth in the seat
   > of the scornful. But his delight is in the
   > law of the Lord; and in his law doth he
   > meditate day and night. (Psalm 1:1–2 KJV)

5. I pray that my offspring be rooted and grounded
   in Christ, that they will be fruitful branches of the
   vine. I pray that they be deeply anchored to Jesus
   and look to Him for everything.

   > Abide in Me, and I in you. As the branch
   > cannot bear fruit of itself, unless it abides

in the vine, neither can you, unless you abide in Me. I am the vine, you are the branches. He who abides in Me, and I in him, bears much fruit; for without Me you can do nothing. (John 15:4–5 KJV)

6. I pray that my son/daughter learns to trust the Lord in everything with all his/her heart and not do things or make decisions based on what seems right by his/her own estimation. The road to perdition and damnation from an independent spirit is not his/her portion in Jesus's name. Amen.

Trust in the Lord with all thine heart; and lean not unto thine own understanding. (Proverbs 3:5 KJV)

7. Son/daughter, keep the commands of the Lord and align to God's will, because He has great things in store for you! He will take you to great heights in the earth.

And it shall come to pass, if thou shalt hearken diligently unto the voice of the Lord thy God, to observe and to do all his commandments which I command thee this day, that the Lord thy God will set thee on high above all nations of the earth. (Deuteronomy 28:1 KJV)

8. Holy Ghost, please guide [insert name] life so that he/she does not give into sinful cravings that would corrupt his/her spirit.

> This I say then, Walk in the Spirit, and ye shall not fulfil the lust of the flesh. (Galatians 5:16 KJV)

9. Lord, give my offspring the strength to face whatever comes their way. May your Spirit help them walk in your power to accomplish all you have called them to, so that they do not continue to strive in their own might.

> Then he answered and spake unto me, saying,This is the word of the Lord unto Zerubbabel, saying, Not by might, nor by power, but by my spirit, saith the Lord of hosts. (Zechariah 4:6 KJV)

10. Son/daughter, I pray that you focus on God who is your only help and not get sidetracked. The Lord will help you always.

> I will lift up mine eyes unto the hills, from whence cometh my help. My help cometh from the Lord, which made heaven and earth. (Psalm 121:1–2 KJV)

11. I pray that my children will grow in grace and knowledge of Jesus. They will align with God's will and be used for his glory till the very end.

> But grow in grace, and in the knowledge of our Lord and Savior Jesus Christ. To him be glory both now and forever. Amen. (2 Peter 3:18 KJV)

12. Thank you, Lord, for rewarding my many nights of praying and crying onto you for my children to return to you and be set free from the grasp of the enemy. My children will live for and serve you, Lord.

> Thus saith the Lord; Refrain thy voice from weeping, and thine eyes from tears: for thy work shall be rewarded, saith the Lord; and they shall come again from the land of the enemy. (Jeremiah 31:16 KJV)

Day 20

ARISE AND SHINE

1. Arise and shine, my child. Your light has come, and God's glory is upon you. In the midst of these dark times, your light will shine through.

   > Arise, shine; for thy light is come, and the glory of the Lord is risen upon thee. For, behold, the darkness shall cover the earth, and gross darkness the people: but the Lord shall arise upon thee, and his glory shall be seen upon thee. (Isaiah 60:1–2 KJV)

2. Son/daughter, God's prophetic word concerning you is definitely sealed. I pray that you focus on it so it will lead you to rise as the morning star in your new season.

   > So we have the prophetic word strongly confirmed. You will do well to pay attention to it, as to a lamp shining in a dismal place, until the day dawns and the morning star rises in your hearts. (2 Peter 1:18–20 HCSB)

3. No enemy will gloat over my offspring. My children will rise from every fall and alight from every dark place because all things will work together for their good. In Jesus's name, amen.

> Rejoice not against me, O mine enemy: when I fall, I shall arise; when I sit in darkness, the Lord shall be a light unto me. (Micah 7:8 KJV)

4. I prophesy to my children that the Spirit of Lord breathe on you and quicken every dead and dying area of your lives in Jesus's name.

> So I prophesied, just as he commanded me. The breath entered them and they came alive! They stood up on their feet, a huge army. (Ezekiel 37:10 MSG)

5. O Lord, give my son/daughter exceptional wisdom and discernment. Expand his/ her mind even as you did for Solomon. May he/she conceive creative and innovate ideas that will change their world.

> And God gave Solomon wisdom and understanding exceeding much, and largeness of heart, even as the sand that is on the sea shore. (1 Kings 4:29 KJV)

Day 21

FOR SIGNS AND WONDERS

1. O Lord, use my children in extraordinary ways that will cause unbelievers to change their mind and believe in you.

   > Behold, I and the children whom the Lord hath given me are for signs and for wonders in Israel from the Lord of hosts, which dwelleth in mount Zion. (Isaiah 8:18 KJV)

2. I declare my offspring are signs of a good future, and their lives reveal Christ and the glory of God.

   > Listen then, Joshua, you who are the High Priest; and listen, you fellow priests of his, you that are the sign of a good future: I will reveal my servant, who is called The Branch! (Zechariah 3:8 GNT)

3. My son/daughter is chosen by God as a symbol of God's purpose on the earth—salvation of souls in their generation and the destruction of the works of darkness.

> And Simeon blessed them, and said unto Mary his mother, Behold, this child is set for the fall and rising again of many in Israel; and for a sign which shall be spoken against. (Luke 2:34 KJV)

4. I declare that [insert name] is a special servant of God called out like Samson from birth to make a godly impact in his/her generation in Jesus's name.

> For, lo, thou shalt conceive, and bear a son; and no razor shall come on his head: for the child shall be a Nazarite unto God from the womb: and he shall begin to deliver Israel out of the hand of the Philistines. (Judges 13:5 KJV)

5. I recognize that my children are special, and they are shining stars. I hide them under the blood of Jesus so the enemy cannot find them.

> The woman became pregnant and gave birth to a son. She saw that he was a special baby and kept him hidden for three months. (Exodus 2:2 NLT)

6. I declare that my children are full of grace, divine blessing, favor, and power, and will do great

miracles and wonders in their generation, in Jesus's name, amen.

> And Stephen, full of faith and power, did great wonders and miracles among the people. (Acts 6:8 KJV)

7. Lord, miraculously send your angels to deliver my son/daughter as you did for the Hebrew boys, and cause their generation to turn to you.

> Then Nebuchadnezzar spake, and said, Blessed be the God of Shadrach, Meshach, and Abednego, who hath sent his angel, and delivered his servants that trusted in him, and have changed the king's word, and yielded their bodies, that they might not serve nor worship any god, except their own God. (Daniel 3:28 KJV)

8. O God, shut the mouth of the lion looking to devour and hurt my children. Protect them and vindicate them, dear Lord.

> My God hath sent his angel, and hath shut the lions' mouths, that they have not hurt me: forasmuch as before him innocency was found in me; and also before thee, O king, have I done no hurt. (Daniel 6:22 KJV)

Printed in the United States
By Bookmasters